SONNY BILL WILLIAMS

A STEP NEARER TO GOD

Crafting Purpose with the Art of Islam

TRANSCRIBED AND ADAPTED FROM
"A STEP NEARER TO GOD: CRAFTING PURPOSE WITH THE ART OF ISLAM"
BY SONNY BILL WILLIAMS & WAEL IBRAHIM

Published by:

Unit No. E-10-5, Jalan SS 15/4G, Subang Square,
47500 Subang Jaya, Selangor, Malaysia
+603-5612-2407 (office) / +6017-399-7411 (mobile)
info@tertib.press
www.tertib.press
@tertibpress (Facebook & Instagram)

Author	:	Sonny Bill Williams
		Wael Ibrahim
Editor / transcriber:		Arisha Mohd Affendy
Cover designer	:	Abdul Adzim Md Daim
Typesetter	:	Abdul Adzim Md Daim
Photographer	:	Muhamad Amirul Johari
		Rafizzul Hazreen

A STEP NEARER TO GOD: CRAFTING PURPOSE WITH THE ART OF ISLAM

First Edition: February 2025

Perpustakaan Negara Malaysia

Cataloguing-in-Publication Data

A catalogue record for this book is available from the National Library of Malaysia

ISBN: 978-967-2844-45-7

Copyright © Sonny Bill Williams, Wael Ibrahim, 2025

All rights reserved.
No part of this publication may be reproduced, distributed, or transmitted in any form or by any means, including photocopying, recording, or other electronic or mechanical methods, without the prior written permission of Tertib Publishing.
Printed in Malaysia.

TABLE OF CONTENTS

Foreword   1
Prologue   2
Being an Athlete and Also a Family Man   4
   An Athlete   6
   A Family Man   8
Life Before Islam   11
   The Turning Point   15
Life After Islam   17
   The Ultimate Trophy   18
   The Backlash   23
   Reactions from Loved Ones   25
From Struggle to Strength   31
Photo Gallery   42
Glossary   50

FOREWORD

Bismillāhirraḥmānirraḥīm

In the name of Allah, the Most Gracious, the Most Merciful.

It is with great honour and gratitude that we present A Step Nearer to God: Crafting Purpose with the Art of Islam, a compelling adaptation of the enlightening dialogue between Sonny Bill Williams and Shaykh Wael, originally shared through the Faith Events talk. This book offers a profound insight into the transformative journey of Sonny Bill Williams, whose faith has become the cornerstone of his life, guiding him from the peak of athletic success to the deep wellspring of spiritual fulfillment.

Through this intimate discussion, readers are invited to explore the path of faith, self-discovery, and purpose that Sonny has walked. His story is one of resilience, humility, and unwavering trust in Allah, and it reminds us that true purpose is not found in external gifts, but in the strength of our connection to the Divine.

Through discipline, devotion, and trust in Allah, we are reminded that this purpose is not a distant ideal but something that can be realised through practical, everyday actions. A key theme of their conversation centers on the hadith of the Prophet Muhammad (SAW): "Tie your camel, then trust in Allah" (Jami' at-Tirmidhi 2517). This timeless wisdom underscores the importance of balancing faith with personal effort, as we strive toward our goals and dreams.

We are deeply thankful to Sonny Bill Williams for sharing his invaluable experiences and insights. May his words inspire readers to take a step nearer to God, finding both strength and purpose in their faith.

In sincere hopes for your progress,

Tertib Publishing.

PROLOGUE

I am not someone who is good at spreading *da'wah*. But, I see this as my duty as a Muslim. The beauty of Islam has made me grow and be a part of things that I never thought possible. So I thought, *khalaṣ*, put the vulnerability hat on, and share my story as a Muslim. Obviously, with the help of Shaykh Wael, I managed to share some gems that have helped me become the person I am.

I was in Malaysia last February for the first time, but previously, I went to perform *'umrah* with my wife—the best experience, *Alḥamdulillāh*. We met three young Malaysian brothers with their family. They were very polite as they came up to me and greeted me with a kiss on my hand, *Mashā'Allāh*. That was one of the reasons why it was easy for me to accept Islam—because of the moral compass that it brings. So my wife and I made the intention that we were going to come to Malaysia sometime soon.

And *Alḥamdulillāh*, I finally came to Malaysia, however, my wife could not come with me back then. But, *Inshā'Allāh*, I will bring her soon.

As the Prophet SAW said:

"Actions are to be judged only by intentions…"

Sunan Abi Dawud 2201

> **So what is the importance of taking action along with good intention?**

For myself, even before Islam, I was always set on growth. I grew up in a house with no wallpaper, and that set me on a path to achieve greater things—materialistically. That was my intention—to achieve status, so that I could buy my mom a house with wallpaper. But *wallāhi*, it was not until I found Islam that I really understood the true meaning of happiness. And I feel like in today's society, as youngsters, we are so fixated on status, negatively. Society pushes in a way where everything is all about flashy cars—wealth, and big arms—appearance. *Wallāhi*, we can achieve all of that, we can strive for that, as long as we have the blessing of Allah SWT, and strive for His sake as well.

I think that is the key—having the mindset to achieve great things, but understanding who gave you the body to do so. Yes, the hadith mentioned above is correct, however, it is not a reference to things that we do on a daily basis. For example: your intention is to go to work, but you did not go. "As long as the intention is there, Allah accepts it and I will get the salary." That is foolish, right?

Hence why the hadith only refers to the acts of worship to Allah SWT. For example: you intended to give charity, but you forgot for some reason. Allah will reward you in the scale of your deeds. But the Prophet SAW said, "If somebody has a good intention and follows it by an action, it would be multiplied by 700 and more folds."

> "...He who intends to do a good deed but he does not do it, then Allah records it for him as a full good deed, but if he carries out his intention, then Allah the Exalted, writes it down for him as from ten to seven hundred folds, and even more..."
>
> Riyaḍ aṣ-Ṣaliḥin 11

That is the true meaning of the real importance of taking action along with your intention.

BEING AN ATHLETE AND ALSO A FAMILY MAN

AN ATHLETE

Being an athlete means that I have to go through a lot of mental training to achieve consistency.

As what Allah SWT mentions:

$$...إِنَّ ٱللَّهَ لَا يُغَيِّرُ مَا بِقَوْمٍ حَتَّىٰ يُغَيِّرُوا۟ مَا بِأَنفُسِهِمْ...$$

...Indeed, Allah will not change the condition of a people until they change what is in themselves...

ar-Raʿd, 13:11

For me and my journey, from where I came to where I am now, it has all been about intentions, and of course, most times, you just have to get it done. Hard work, perseverance, *ṣabr*. These are all lessons—the teachings that I have learnt and highlighted once I became a Muslim. And the outcome is upon Allah SWT. So just do your part and Allah SWT will bless that effort.

My favourite motto is *#alwaysAlhamdulillāh*. I also have a saying on the wall that says, "tie the camel up." It is from the hadith where the *ṣaḥabah* asked the Prophet SAW if he should tie the camel, and the Prophet said to put trust in Allah, but tie the camel up too.

Anas ibn Malik reported:

A man said, "O' Messenger of Allah, should I tie my camel and trust in Allah, or should I leave her untied and trust in Allah?" The Prophet, peace and blessings be upon him, said, "Tie her and trust in Allah."

Jamiʿ at-Tirmidhi 2517

> This is my life. Every day I try to do my daily routine, as simple as it is, as mundane as it is, whether it being with my wife or my kids, *Alḥamdulillāh*. And once I am done, I will put my trust in Allah SWT.

A FAMILY MAN

> Aside from being an athlete and taking care or looking after yourself, you are also responsible for your wife and children—you are a family man. You teared up in one of the videos when your children came from school. How does it feel to be a family man? After all, the highlights are on you and your family now.

> I think I try to act the way the Prophet SAW acts—he SAW embraced his vulnerabilities and the trials and tribulations that he went through.

As for myself, as a sportsman and a rugby man, I have to be the tough guy, since there is true power and strength in embracing those qualities as well. So, that is what I try to do. But, I think the beauty of Islam has allowed me to understand that it is OK to be a man and show emotions, and that it is OK to be a man and cry. Even when doing the chores around the house, I sometimes show my emotions, but I have really come to understand and appreciate that, and just try my best in the house. That is also the recipe for happiness at home—expressing my emotions, and spending time with my family.

There was this one time when I tried to prove to my wife that women tend to do things the hard way—they tend to complicate things—but after trying to prove to her, I realised that it took me the same amount of time as her. Because of that 'debate', I came to the conclusion that unless you share your wife's interest and unless your wife shares your interest, there will be no happiness. I think for couples out there, the thing that has really helped me in my marriage is understanding our weaknesses, and understanding that we are both not perfect humans. And when I really understood this and stepped into that, our relationship started to thrive.

$$...\text{وَعَسَىٰٓ أَن تَكْرَهُوا۟ شَيْـًٔا وَهُوَ خَيْرٌ لَّكُمْ ۖ وَعَسَىٰٓ أَن تُحِبُّوا۟ شَيْـًٔا وَهُوَ شَرٌّ لَّكُمْ ۗ}...$$

...But perhaps you hate a thing and it is good for you; and perhaps you love a thing and it is bad for you...

al-Baqarah, 2:216

We all want to feel important as people, so do our wives. So take care of them and love them, but understand that they have their wants, pleasures and cares—the things that they find exciting, and in turn she does things for me as well. And I think that is the process and the beauty of Islam because we were taught that it is not just about ourselves. 'Give and you will receive.' So it has really helped with my household. Sometimes it has been a little bit frustrating, but this is what life is all about. It is not easy, but you have to go through these hassles.

LIFE BEFORE ISLAM

> **Before Islam, were you also religious? Were you keen to practise any faith? And how does this feel back then?**

Growing up, I had always believed in God, just like every Polynesian islanders. The majority of the brothers and sisters there are of Christian faith and although in my household we were not really practising any faith, I would classify myself as a Christian just because all my close friends were islanders.

Ever since I was a child, I was always fixated on buying a house with wallpapers for my mom since I came from nothing. When I was 18, *Alḥamdulillāh*, I was able to buy mom a house. I was recognised as one of the best players in the world at that time. But after tasting success and fame, I had a 'what if' moment. I knew I needed more purpose. Just like when Shaykh Wael had when the brother committed suicide, that was my 'what if' moment. Going from relatively unknown to becoming very famous overnight, people coming up to me asking for signatures and photos, really puts me in a path of purpose. I realised that when it comes to materialistic things, even after receiving them, you are still not happy. Yes, I was playing really well, I bought mom a house, but then what's next? I started going into hiding, I went into a dark place. Because I felt like I was missing something. That was when I started reading self-help books and going back to the church. One day, I met some brothers that I always see at a local cafe near my house. They would hang out and congregate there and would pray together. They told me about Islam, and that was the most content I felt for a long time. But I was still living the other life. Despite them telling me about Islam—about *Alḥamdulillāh*, *SubḥānAllāh*, *Bismillāh*—I still lived my other life on the side. *Astaghfirullāh*.

I was partying, taking drugs, womanising, *Astaghfirullāh*, all of these things. And in reality, all I was searching for was purpose. And then *Alḥamdulillāh*, Islam came. I do not know why in France though, I am still trying to wrap my head around this. But I learned more about the beauty of Islam in France. I got to know a Tunisian family who lived ten minutes away from me there. I spent most of my time there sleeping on the floor with the boys, learning about Islam, learning about the love they had within their household through actions. And I have always been a person who learns through actions more so than words. And that was where I found the beauty of Islam—through their actions, and then obviously with that, I wanted more. And that was where I went down the path of trying to upskill myself from a knowledge point. It was very difficult. After embracing Islam, despite knowing that the media will tarnish my image—the public's perception—it was all still worth it.

The feeling of happiness one gets when they are in *sujud*, or even seeing the goodness of Islam through actions, I could not deny it. And when I was searching for purpose, being a man of faith, I always believe the beauty of Islam is the way that Muslims revere their faith. The way that Muslims cherish being Muslims. And that was what I was drawn into. The way the brothers conducted themselves and the way that their way of life reflected their beliefs. So I just pushed the public backlash to the side, because the feeling I got of happiness, I could not get that anywhere else. And obviously with the good company around me to support and assist me.

> I must admit, the battle is not easy—the battle against *shayṭan* is not easy, the battle against yourself, your own desires, is not easy. But one of the most important elements that keeps people steadfast is actually the righteous company.

Allah SWT describes this in surah al-Kahf:

وَٱصْبِرْ نَفْسَكَ مَعَ ٱلَّذِينَ يَدْعُونَ رَبَّهُم بِٱلْغَدَوٰةِ وَٱلْعَشِيِّ يُرِيدُونَ وَجْهَهُۥ ۖ وَلَا تَعْدُ عَيْنَاكَ عَنْهُمْ تُرِيدُ

زِينَةَ ٱلْحَيَوٰةِ ٱلدُّنْيَا ۖ وَلَا تُطِعْ مَنْ أَغْفَلْنَا قَلْبَهُۥ عَن ذِكْرِنَا وَٱتَّبَعَ هَوَىٰهُ وَكَانَ أَمْرُهُۥ فُرُطًا ﴿٢٨﴾

And keep yourself patient [by being] with those who call upon their Lord in the morning and the evening, seeking His face [i.e., acceptance]. And let not your eyes pass beyond them, desiring adornments of the worldly life, and do not obey one whose heart We have made heedless of Our remembrance and who follows his desire and whose affair is ever [in] neglect.

al-Kahf, 18:28

When you see those people, do not let your eyes stray away from them. Speak to them because they will always drag you back upon the true path. Surround yourself with those people. Listen to what they have to say. Ask them questions, debate with them, but do it in a good manner. Wisdom—beautiful preaching and argument in the best way possible. You may argue and debate, but do it in the best manner, as manners are a part of Islam. We are not belittling the act of worship, but look at the level of manners. Mannerism—good-hearted people, mercy, generosity. The Prophet SAW said:

"The dearest and the closest of you to me on the Day of Resurrection will be those who are the best in behaviour; and the most hateful and the farthest from me on the Day of Resurrection will be the talkative and the most pretentious and the most rhetorical."

Riyaḍ aṣ-Ṣaliḥin 1738

THE TURNING POINT

> For the benefit of those of us who might be experiencing an opportunity where a non-Muslim is maybe on the verge of joining Islam, could you give an example of the actions that you witnessed with your Tunisian friend that sort of drove you to embrace Islam?

What led me to Islam was I wanted what I saw, plain and simple, and what I saw was happiness, contentment, brotherhood, a life which showcased their beliefs wholeheartedly, and that was what I wanted

Three months ago, I met a brother that I had not seen for a very long time. I actually played at the highest level with him. We caught up, we talked, and started talking about Islam. He was a man of faith as well. I gave him a little book. Three months later, he reverted to Islam—he became a Muslim. I helped a little bit, but I cannot claim all of it. *SubḥānAllāh*, there have been multiple people that I have tried to help so many times for so long, but it did not work.

I guess my answer in short is do your best, lead through actions, but understand that Allah guides whom He wills. Even the Prophet's uncle did not accept Islam, despite being with the Prophet.

LIFE AFTER ISLAM

THE ULTIMATE TROPHY

> Now you have carried and lifted many trophies and many awards in the past. Tell me about the one trophy that says, *Lā ĩlāha ĩlla-llāh, Muḥammadur-Rasūlu-llāh.* I think the ultimate trophy is when you accept Islam, in your *shahadah*. What was your feeling the moment you recited the *kalimah*?

So for those that did not know my story, I went through a time in my life where the way I was living felt like it would eventually lead to a dead end, or something equally dire. So I decided—while I was in a five-year contract—to leave. I broke my contract. And on that day when I went to France, I was fearful, anxious. But the brother that I was learning a lot of Islam through, just said to me, "Would you like to make your *shahadah*?" I did not know what was going on in my head, but I said, "Yes, of course." And I made that *shahadah*. It was weird, it felt kind of surreal when I looked back into it. I did not feel like, "Oh, I am saved." But I almost felt like from that moment on, I had the courage to just walk and say, *Lā ĩlāha ĩlla-llāh, Muḥammadur-Rasūlu-llāh*, despite the consequences of breaking the contract, which was tied to a big amount of money.

I ended up in a million dollars debt because I had to pay a big bill. But from that moment on, I always say, *Alḥamdulillāh*. That was where "always *Alḥamdulillāh*" came from. I went through a lot of struggles, even after I accepted Islam, probably more so. But the beauty of Islam is that it has given me things in my life that when that stormy weather hits, I can deal with it. Allah is there. *Alḥamdulillāh*.

My mother's revert story is based on the Christchurch mosque attacks. May Allah have mercy on all their souls. As a Muslim, I had to speak up about it. When I got back home, I spoke to my mother and she said to me, "I don't know if there are any other people that could hold their nerve and show such strength as the Muslims do at this time." Then we carried on the conversation, then she said, "You know, if I am to choose a religion or be Islam, well then I'd jump straight on that." And she said her *shahadah* right then and there.

After that incident, there were many reversions in New Zealand. Non-Muslims were not happy with what happened. It was terrible. But sometimes, situations like this are out of our control. Like the situation I encountered that one time, where a girl came up from behind me and started hugging me. She was crying. I froze, I did not know what to say or do. But it's just as simple as these elements that you show to non-Muslims and others, that can actually draw their attention to Islam.

I always think from a revert's point of view too. I remember the first time I went to Dubai, as a Muslim, thinking, "I'm here, in my brother and sister's country." But when I stepped into the masjid, the brother turned me away because I had a tattoo. He said, "You can't come in unless you take those off first."

My point of the story is that, from a revert's perspective, for those who were born Muslims, and know their faith well, please live with empathy, because your actions speak louder than words. Because that was what drew me to Islam, and I know that that is what draws a lot of people to Islam too—our actions.

Shaykh Wael's additional comments:

Obviously, that was wrong, but these tattoos are a reminder of the dark stage of your life that you went through. And every time you look at it, say *Alḥamdulillāh* that Allah gave you the opportunity to embrace Islam before it was too late.

Islam erases whatever comes before it. Whatever you have done before the repentance, once you have repented, those moments are erased completely. So do not wait for it. Take those actions before it is too late. That is what is going to help you get better and better, *Inshā'Allāh*.

> **How did you first start learning about praying and how did you remain consistent?**

One of the things that got me really connected to Islam about was, at that time, I believed I was a Christian. I understood and loved the fact that 'Isa AS (Jesus) was our God. It was actually a moment of clarity for me as I began to wonder, "Whose household would 'Isa want to be in?" And I thought to myself, "How did Jesus actually pray?"

That set me on a path of learning. Because I simply just wanted to improve, and the empowerment that I got when I learned, "Oh, not only the pious predecessors prayed like this, but the greatest people of all time prayed like this too." *SubḥānAllāh*, it was just a journey of upskilling myself, and with that grind and hard work in improving, came empowerment. I could not really push it to the side anymore, that was what I wanted eventually. That was how I started to learn how to pray.

Shaykh Wael's additional comments:

And the root word of *ṣalah* is *ṣilah*—connection. Building our connection with Allah SWT. It is the most important pillar of the *dīn* of Allah SWT. Everything can be exempted; your *zakah*, if you do not have the means, then you do not need to pay them. If you cannot go for *ḥajj*, then you do not have to. But there is no excuse for *ṣalah*. Once you have reached the age of puberty, and you are sane—you know how to reason, then there is no excuse. If you are sick, you pray while sitting. If you cannot sit, lie down. I remember my father's last day, he prayed using his fingers, he would do the position with his finger, because that was all that he could move.

So, there is no excuse. May Allah SWT make us grounded with this connection with Him to become a better Muslim.

You mentioned your struggle of reciting surah al-Fatiḥah. My wife is a Filipino, her Arabic is not perfect up until now, but remember the hadith where the Prophet SAW said that, "Those who read the Qu'ran fluently will get one reward, and those who read it with a struggle will get a double reward."

> The Prophet SAW said, "Such a person as recites the Qu'ran and masters it by heart, will be with the noble righteous scribes (in Heaven). And such a person exerts himself to learn the Qu'ran by heart, and recites it with great difficulty, will have a double reward."
>
> Ṣaḥīḥ al-Bukhari 4937

So do not fear saying it in the wrong way, you will be corrected, of course, but do not worry if you are struggling. As long as you are serious about your *ṣalah*, you will get double the reward.

Sonny Bill Williams: *Wallāhi*, for my journey as a revert, it is quite intimidating meeting brothers like Shaykh Wael, but when you understand the *ḥikmah*—the wisdom of the Prophet SAW, his sayings, *subḥānAllāh*. It puts ease in your heart, knowing that that struggle is a blessing, and you are rewarded for it, *Alḥamdulillāh*.

THE BACKLASH

> **So talk to us about the worst backlash you have received after your *shahadah*. And how did you deal with it?**

I think I even remember my father saying, "What are you doing? Why?" Some close friends of mine at that time dispersed, left. But *Alḥamdulillāh*, when you step into that space wholeheartedly, you meet new friends. You surround yourself with new people—that you should be surrounding yourself with in the first place. I always consider myself so lucky because of the path that I was on, and then Allah chose me for this beautiful religion, and led me in a way where not only can I take those lessons that I have had in life, but I can preach it and I can give it to others.

The Prophet SAW said:

"A man is upon the religion of his best friend, so let one of you look at whom he befriends."

Jamiʿ at-Tirmidhi 2378

So any brothers and sisters out there who are struggling with things or know that they should not be doing certain things, look at your closest companions. Look at your inner circle with the sincerest intentions. Look at what changes them, and you will change yourself too. Those backlashes will remain there, but because you have the support of those around you, you will not care for the judgement.

Other than that, you need to also set some boundaries. I thrive by putting boundaries on my life knowing my own frailties. For example: the *fitnah* of social media. I have my wife that runs all my socials. Because I know, I understand the struggle of sitting there scrolling, potentially looking at things you should not look at. So I simply just ask my wife to manage it, *Alḥamdulillāh*.

> **But how does your wife deal with the comments and the dms on your social media?**

Sometimes, I come home from work or whatever it may be, and I can tell that my wife is just in that mood and something is up. So I know something is up. Turns out it is because of some comments such as, "Oh, you look good."

But I think that is just part and parcel of life, and *Alḥamdulillāh*, the closer that me and my wife have gotten together to Allah and work on our relationship with Allah, the happier we have been.

This is a very important lesson for everyone here who admire people in the spotlight and contact them and appreciate them. Put some boundaries, because *wallāhi* you may lead others to destruction. Be responsible, and be careful. We are human beings. We have our own shortcomings. We have our own problems. So do not multiply these problems. Be responsible when you contact people you know who are of that class.

REACTIONS FROM LOVED ONES

> **How did your All Blacks brothers react to you embracing Islam? And All Blacks, the rugby game is a huge mindset game, right? So how did you step up, you know, your mind game to overcome all those challenges, but still perform and win?**

Did you know that there is a Muslim brother who is still in All Blacks? *Alḥamdulillāh*, he still plays.

But I think I have always never shied away from being a Muslim. I have always been proud to be a Muslim. And whether I was in the All Blacks system or in another team, I always put my heart on my sleeve. And if you like me, you like me. If you don't, *khalaṣ*. But I strive to always lead through my actions and be a good person. And I think that the brothers respected that because at the end of the day, I still wanted to win. And I always take that mindset into whatever I try to do.

I think the beauty of Islam, becoming a Muslim, is how you improve based on what Islam teaches us. It starts with having a positive mindset which leaks through into our actions. And that was what came natural to me as a sportsman. I was always trying to improve. I just changed that to Islam. And that is why I am able to get to where I am right now. I am still striving, still learning, *Alḥamdulillāh*. And that is what Islam teaches us—to continue to grow.

> **After reverting, how do you readjust yourself to your surroundings—your family, your friends?**

Shaykh Wael's additional comments:

I observed a lot of Filipino sisters who came to Islam, and they were working with non-Muslims in Hong Kong City in particular, and it was very difficult for them to practise Islam. Now, they took their *shahadah*—the first step, but practising the faith—putting the *hijab* on, praying on time, that they were struggling. Some of the employers were actually prohibiting them, forbidding them from praying. So, did you experience something similar to that?

Sonny Bill Williams: Of course, even to this day. I love what you said Shaykh, about being serious, no one loves you like you love yourself. No one wants the best for you other than yourself. So, I was on that path of taking things seriously. The beautiful brothers who were teaching me Islam, they gave me a simple instruction, which I think is powerful for all of us when faced with a revert or someone new to the religion or wanting to get involved with the religion. Give them a simple instruction which is, "Work on your relationship with Allah SWT, build your knowledge and understand that it is a marathon, not a sprint." And with that mindset, it really worked wonders for me.

I have never been the greatest at school, at learning, but I understood with just perseverance, it builds my connection with Allah SWT. *Alḥamdulillāh.*

Shaykh Wael's additional comments:

Yes, step by step is really important. I have seen a lot of people that as soon as they embrace Islam, the brothers and sisters around them want to help them to learn, but sometimes they overload them with a lot of things that make these people overwhelmed. So take it easy on people, be merciful, and remember if you teach anyone a letter of the Qur'an or how to pray, and those people persistently pray, every *rakʿah* will be rewarded.

"He who introduced some good practice in Islam which was followed after him (by people) he would be assured of reward like one who followed it, without their rewards being diminished in any respect…"

Ṣaḥīḥ Muslim 1017e

> Once it hits your heart, everything becomes easy, *SubḥānAllāh*. When I first reverted, I overthought a lot, "What about this? What about that?" But once the beauty of Islam hits your heart, it is game over. So that is a little bit of an insight when dealing with people trying to get into the *dīn*. Just wait for it to hit you in the heart.

Shaykh Wael's additional comments:

Our job is to convey, to assist and to help, but Allah is the One who will open the heart for others.

$$\text{إِنَّكَ لَا تَهْدِى مَنْ أَحْبَبْتَ وَلَـكِنَّ ٱللَّهَ يَهْدِى مَن يَشَآءُ} \ldots$$

Indeed, [O' Muḥammad], you do not guide whom you like, but Allah guides whom He wills…

al-Qaṣaṣ, 28:56

So be merciful, and do not ever mock others for not doing what you are doing. In fact, you should always remember the *duʿāʾ* of the Prophet SAW:

$$...\text{ٱلْحَمْدُ لِلَّهِ ٱلَّذِى هَدَىٰنَا لِهَٰذَا وَمَا كُنَّا لِنَهْتَدِىَ لَوْلَا أَنْ هَدَىٰنَا ٱللَّهُ}...$$

...'Praise to Allah, who has guided us to this; and we would never have been guided if Allah had not guided us...'

al-A'raf, 7:43

So the guidance is from Allah SWT. When you see someone who is not praying, not waking up for *fajr*, do not try to feel like you are the better person. Instead, pray for them, and pray that you stay *istiqamah*.

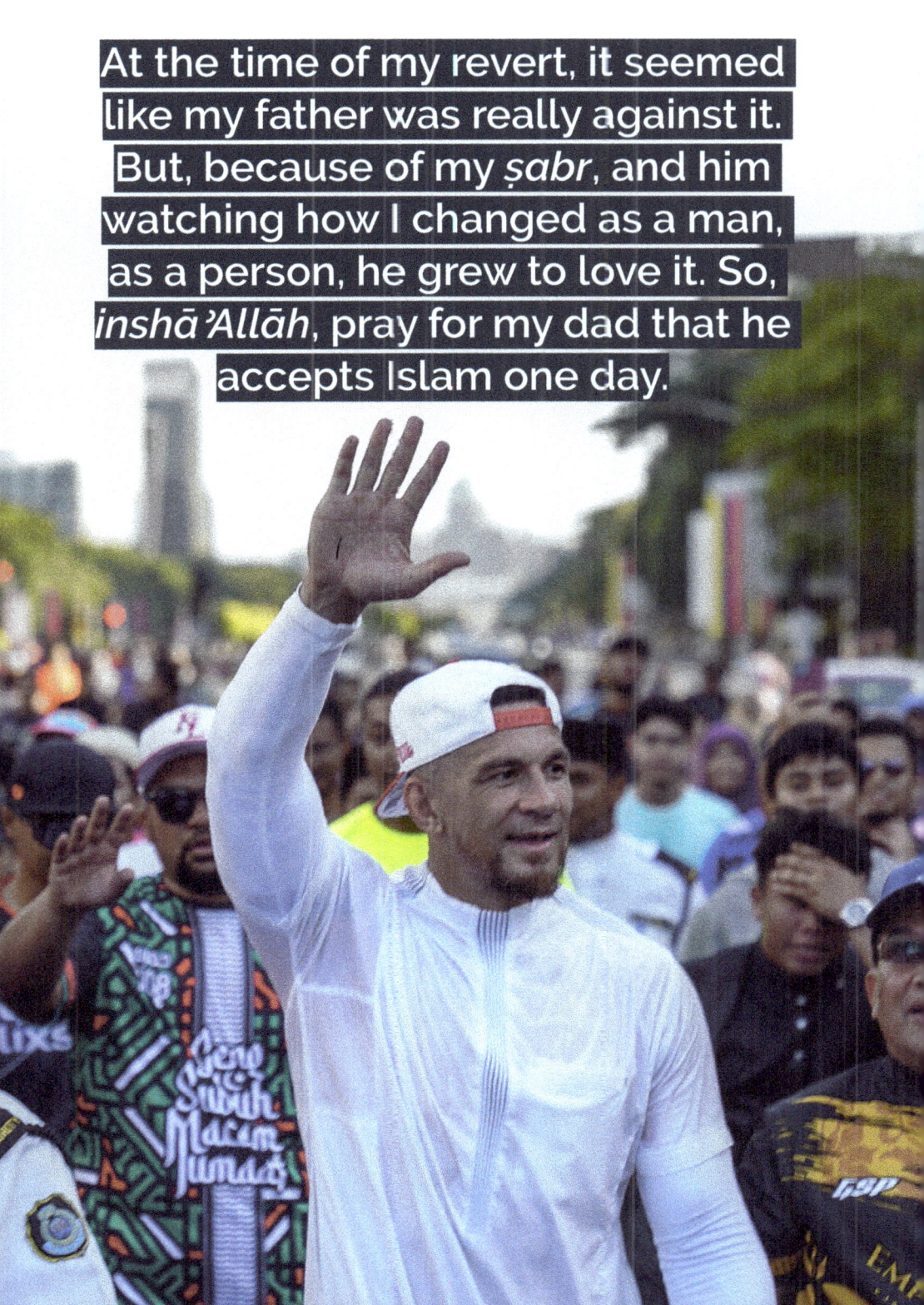

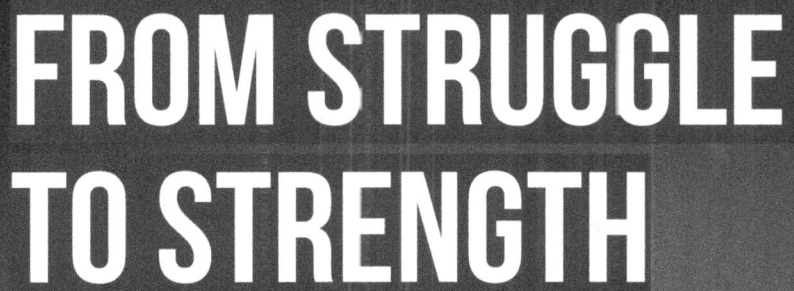
FROM STRUGGLE TO STRENGTH

> **What is your lowest point for your life before and after Islam? And how does it differ with one another—what is your connection with your relationship between both?**

So my lowest point before Islam was also my highest point. Imagine a young boy who had nothing and strove his best, and finally got it—at such a young age; wealth, status, pleasing the family. As that time came, that young boy suddenly sat and thought, "Man, I've achieved what I've set out to achieve in life. What now?" So at that moment of time, all I got were questions. I kept on questioning things. After a while, it set me on a path to where I am now—finding a purpose, *Alḥamdulillāh*.

Post Islam, as a Muslim, I find hardships all the time. A while back, I lost my first fight in the boxing ring. And because I was a high-performing sportsman for so long, my fear of losing was the embarrassment that I would put on my family for not being perfect and it was such a hard time, but *Alḥamdulillāh*, Allah showed me that true strength comes from Allah SWT, and not myself. So I went through that hardship and the beauty of that hardship was learning that I needed to work on my relationship with Allah SWT.

Shaykh Wael's additional comments:

So, at one point, you were fighting and doing sports, while also pleasing others, and that put a lot of pressure. Actually, many of us do that. We do not have one person to judge us, to talk about us. So, we work and live for others, and forget about ourselves. But when you direct this to "I will just work this with Allah, and focus on what He wants me to achieve, then things will be easier."

Sonny Bill Williams: For sure, and I think that that happens to all of us. We get caught up in this *dunya* in what we are doing. We have good intentions, trying to achieve something for our family. But along that way, we suddenly lose the fact of why we are really trying to achieve it. That was what happened in my life at the time, I was so busy and I got caught up, and then, Allah taught me a lesson.

> **What is the reaction between you and your wife in answering the hatred in the social media commenting that you have forced your wife and kids to wear the *ḥijab*?**

Seeing my wife putting on a *ḥijab* was one of the proudest moments of my life, because I went through a phase where when I started learning more about Islam—I started becoming more religious. And because I was on that journey, I expected those close to me to be on the same journey as me. So I started putting pressure on my wife to put a headscarf on, and *subḥānAllāh*, my wife being the feisty Cape Malay that she is, told me, "Look, this is my journey, you worry about yourself and stop pointing fingers." So *subḥānAllāh*, I just went on my own journey. I understand that I am the shepherd of my own family and I have to lead by actions, and that was how I always did when I was a rugby player—leading by actions, and *subḥānAllāh*, I forgot about it.

Three years later, when I got back from my *fajr* prayer at the masjid, I sat downstairs and wondered where my wife was, because she was usually downstairs. When I got up to our room, I found her praying and crying, so I waited for her to finish her prayer, thinking to myself, "What did I do?" After she finished praying, she turned to me and told me, "Today is the day, it's time."

My point of this story is for us men, yes, we are the leader of the household. But there is a responsibility on you to lead through your actions and be authentic in it. Because everyone can smell when you are not doing it properly. And if I can give a bit of advice, it is to be authentic in leading through your actions because the women will follow you.

> Do you have any difficulties while learning Islam? Because I am from Japan, I am still learning Islam and I realised that the Islam community in Japan is still a minority.

Shaykh Wael's additional comments:

I visited Japan recently and went to almost every mosque—every place of worship—in Japan. Every time I go there, believe it or not, there is a majority of the Japanese Islam community. You know what that means? It means that if you want to surround yourself with a specific circle, that circle will become your majority. You will see them all the time, I actually felt like I belonged in Japan. Plus, the Japanese community is almost Muslim, without the *shahadah*. I actually have a topic called 'Japan and Islam', with evidence that everything that they are doing—their mannerism—has Islamic roots. Hence, you would make a very good Muslim. Because you will not change your roots, your behaviour, your manners. All you will do is acknowledging the One who made you. Do you believe that there is One being who created you, fashioned you? If you believe that, then you are 50%, and the second 50% is when Allah SWT sent the Messengers to teach you how to connect with the Creator who made you. If you acknowledge this, then you are a 100% Muslim, *inshā'Allāh*.

So believe me it is a lifelong learning process, this does not happen overnight. There will definitely be a lot of adjustments and challenges. If you believe with all your heart—even if it is just 1%—that God is the One who created this universe, and that Muḥammad SAW is the final Messenger, the most important thing you can do is saying your **shahadah**. Do not walk away without saying your **shahadah**. This is your learning process. Seek any Islamic community and ask for their help and assistance to grow your faith in Islam, bit by bit.

> **Can you share some of your good experiences during 'umrah and Ramadan?**

The first time I went to *'umrah* was in 2015, and my senses were just overloaded. I did not know what was going on, I had little knowledge at that time—I still do now too. But, from that little hardship, I was embarrassed that I did not know much and that put me on a little bit of a path to learn about the *ṣaḥabah*, how strong and powerful they were. I went back to *'umrah* with my wife in 2023, and that was one of the best experiences of my life. My wife saw the Ka'bah for the first time, and I asked her, "How are you feeling my love?" She said, "I'm home. I'm where I'm meant to be." *Alḥamdulillāh*, that was one of the best moments of my life—along with when my mom became a Muslim. That is the beauty of Islam—it ticks all the boxes that our natural inclinations want and yearn for.

What I love and am proud of being a Muslim is that we live a life with boundaries, and try to improve ourselves everyday. That is why we should always say *"Alḥamdulillāh"*, that Allah wakes us up as Muslims. Because there are too many people in the world who are proud to live a life that has got no boundaries. And that is what I really love about being a Muslim, *Alḥamdulillāh*.

Shaykh Wael's additional comments:

Yes, the experience of seeing the Ka'bah for the first time is amazing. My wife and I went for our *'umrah* in 2015 too, and my wife was a fresh Muslim at that time, and she started crying as soon as she entered the Ka'bah. She had never been there before, she did not know much about the history of Ka'bah, but she cried. Later I asked her why, and she said that the peace—the inner peace that surrounded her was inexplainable. May Allah SWT grant everyone the ability to go and enjoy the surroundings of the Ka'bah.

> **When All Blacks won the 2015 Rugby World Cup, you gave away your winning medal to this one lucky fan. Why did you give away something that you have worked hard for? What came into your mind that moment?**

I do not have any of my memorabilia to be honest, and I think that is a blessing that Allah gave me. I came from nothing, and I know that I will leave here with nothing. My management team is always on me to be better at my finances and such. But I see that as a blessing, I do not hold on to things. When it comes to that young brother, he got tackled and he looked hurt, so my empathetic heart felt sorry for him. So I took him back to his family, and just to make his day, I gave him my medal. And until this day, *subḥānAllāh*, this young brother who received my medal has dedicated his life to do a charity—doing a good cause—around that medal. So we never know what good deeds come of things we give people. *Alḥamdulillāh*.

Shaykh Wael's additional comments:

Mashā'Allāh, that reminds me of an *ayah*:

$$\text{لَن تَنَالُوا۟ ٱلْبِرَّ حَتَّىٰ تُنفِقُوا۟ مِمَّا تُحِبُّونَ} ...$$

Never will you attain the good [reward] until you spend [in the way of Allah] from that which you love…

Ali-'Imran, 3:92

Something that you are attached to in this *dunya*, learn to give it away. *Wallāhi*, Allah will give you even more. I remember a brother of mine, I visited his home once and as I hugged him, I smelled his perfume. Mind you, I am a perfume addict. I love fine perfume. Everyone has a weakness, and mine is a perfume. My wife always warns me not to buy expensive perfume whenever I travel.

When I smelled that fine perfume, I said, "Wow, that perfume smells really nice." That was all I said, and we continued our night as if nothing had happened. When I was about to leave, he dropped the perfume bottle into my pocket, and said, "That's yours." Later on, I realised that it was a very expensive perfume, and it was one of his favourite perfumes. Sometimes it is very difficult to give up our favourite things—things that we love.

Most people, when they want to donate some money to others, sometimes they reach into their pockets and take out things. They try to separate the rubbish and some leftover money that they manage to fish out of their pockets, and donate that money—the money that you will never use since it has long been in your pocket, most people will most likely give that to charity, donating that money.

> **But it is quite the opposite with Islam where you give the best out of what you have, if you really believe that the One who actually gave you that is Allah SWT. So the more you give of Allah's provision, the more He will give you.**

There is a hadith that said:

"None of you believes until he loves for his brother what he loves for himself."

Jami' at-Tirmidhi 2515

That is a very good mindset, but when you strive to do that, that is empowering, especially when you feel the love coming back to you. A lot of people do not understand the *barakah* in that. They always think of themselves.

> **What is your advice to those people who are on the verge of making a change, but they are waiting, or are tired of the reaction of the people in their midst?**

I think, in life, the enemy of making change is the perfect outcome—thinking that it is going to be perfect. But, *wallāhi*, start! Put your vulnerability hat on and just get up and start. In my life, I came from nothing. I had everything that I dreamed of and I still felt nothing. Not until I became a Muslim, did I understand the true understanding of what gives me that happiness. And it is my relationship with my Creator. There were many times where I was in *sujud*, making *du'a'*, and tears just came rolling down my face because as Muslims, of course we will understand the power of Allah SWT—the blessings of our life, just from our eyes, from our lips, from our tongue.

What I am trying to say is, no one will make that change for you, you have to do it yourself. When you take a step towards Him SWT, He will come running to you. His blessings will come, just be sincere.

> "He who comes closer to Me one span, I come closer to him a cubit; and he who comes closer to Me a cubit, I come closer to him a fathom; and if he comes to Me walking, I come to him running."
>
> Riyaḍ aṣ-Ṣaliḥin 440

The Prophet SAW mentioned before:

"...Stick to the group of Muslims and their Imam (ruler)..."

Ṣaḥiḥ al-Bukhari 7084

But do not think that once you become a Muslim, your life will be rosy and happy. You will be tested a lot more after. Because Allah SWT will test those who are sincere.

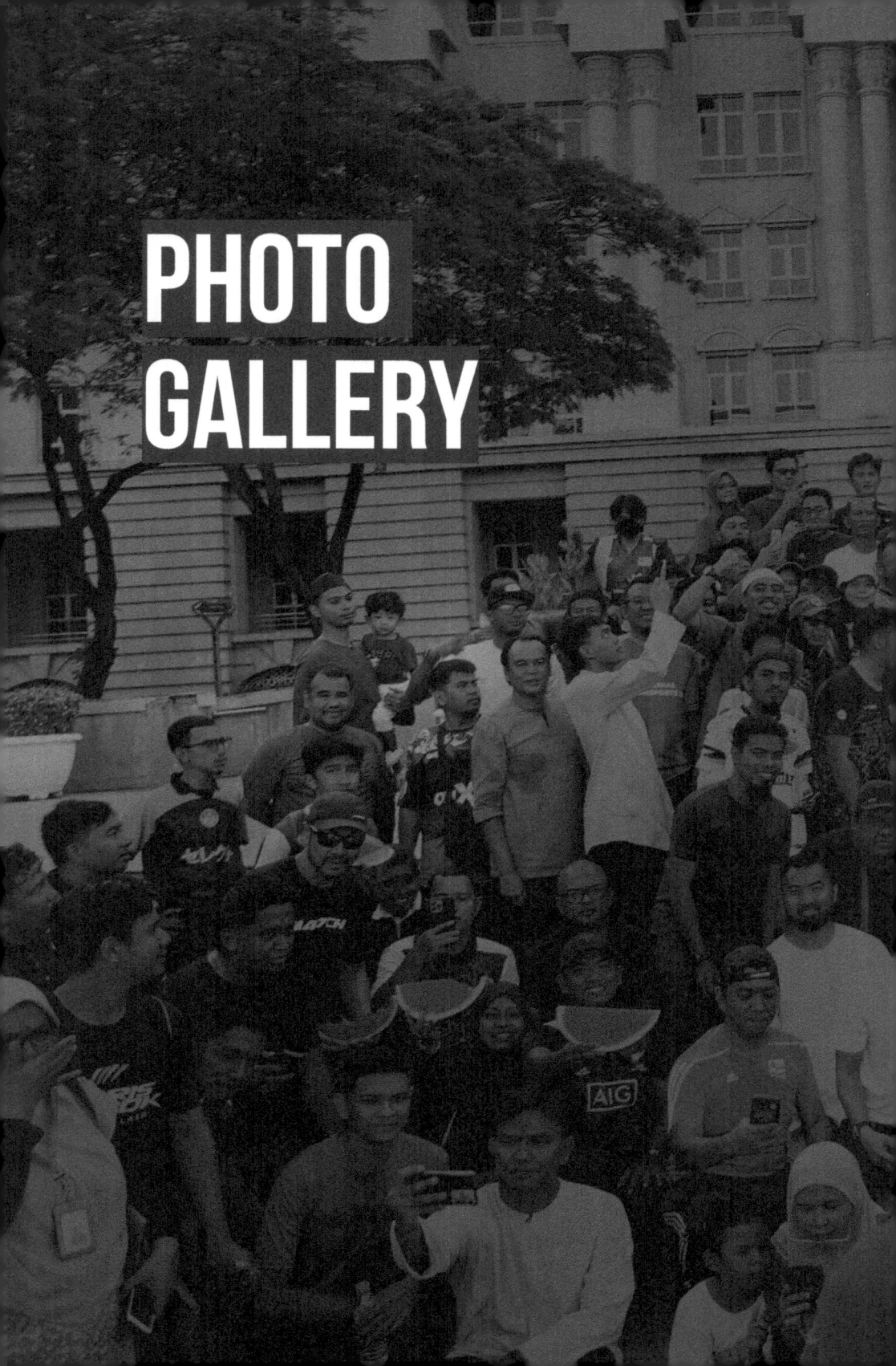

GLOSSARY

Alḥamdulillāh - Praise be to Allah

Astaghfirullāh - I seek forgiveness in Allah

Ayah - Verse

Bismillāh - In the name of Allah

Daʿwah - A call to embrace Islam

Dīn - Religion

Duʿaʾ - Supplication

Dunya - Worldly

Fajr - Dawn

Fitnah - Temptation

Ḥajj - Pilgrimage to Makkah

Ḥijab - Veil

Ḥikmah - Wisdom

InshāʾAllāh - If Allah wills

Istiqamah - Steadfastness

Kalimah - Word

Khalaṣ - Enough

Lā ʾilāha ʾilla-llāh - There is no deity worthy of worship or unconditional obedience except Allah

MashāʾAllāh - As Allah has willed

Rakʿah - Bow/A single iteration of prescribed movements and supplications

Ṣabr - Perserverance

Ṣaḥabah - Companions

Ṣalah - Prayers
Shahadah - Profession of faith
Shayṭan - The Devil
Ṣilah - Connection
SubḥānAllāh - Glory be to Allah
Sujud - Prostration
ʿUmrah - Lesser pilgrimage
Wallāhi - I swear to Allah
Zakah - Charity

www.ingramcontent.com/pod-product-compliance
Lightning Source LLC
LaVergne TN
LVHW061631070526
838199LV00071B/6648